Copyrigl

I AM BIRMINGHAM

The Peoples Poet

Jamil Glenn

Kindle Direct Publishing

"A GEM FOR YOUR SOUL"

I speak into souls
Riding Box Chevy's and Cadillac's
I speak into souls
Living in the projects or a one room shack
I speak into souls
That feel trapped
Trapped by society
Trapped by the American Judicial System
Bound by the letter of Willie Lynch
Held captive by a mental glitch
Drowning sorrows with a couple sips
Trying to elevate from a place with a hit of a lit blunt
Incarcerated mentally replaying the words from a
mother to her son
Life ain't been no crystal stair
For black teens with dreams of cream, riding clean,
with gold and diamonds that bling
Ask yourself, why does the caged bird really sing
Roll of thunder hear our cry
Hear the cry of the little boy sleep off lean
Hear the cry of the little boy that believe the lies of a
crafty team
Hear the cry of a mother that cries over the little boy
that blood streams through the streets of the city
The end results of a menace to society
A boy in the hood inspired by those that grip wood
and ride with steel
With a mother trying to move on up that hill

Trying to provide a hot meal
Trying to find peace through her veins and a pill
Trying to make ends with a red dress and heels
The rich stay rich and live
The poor remains broke dying to live and living to
survive
It's a fight to stay alive
Because no one wants to die
That's why many get high
Pray first then ride
It's all out genocide
The last leaf on the limb
Your life is a hymn
Out of your pain and struggle your soul is
being formed into the perfect gem

"THE GENEALOGY OF ME"

Columbus, Mississippi
Where my family roots reside
Birmingham, Alabama
Born and raised
From the West side
Forever I rise
I live to transition into the next life
Southern rooted to the core
In a distant land stolen from the Indians and Moors
America, America, do you really want a civil war
Our melanin is protected by the Sword of the Lord
Followed by an ancestral encore
No eye has seen, and no ear has heard what the Lord
has in store
Revolutionaries are not afraid of blood and gore
Why live in fear? When in death you sore
Whats a golden crown
To an Earthly reward
What's a golden calf
To deep wounds and battles scars
Always keep your heart
Never compromise your art
For a will to shine and ball
What does it profit a man
To gain it all
And forfeit his own soul
For a glorification of something that want go
When his soul transitions through the universe

Among the stars and the planets
Into the next life
The realm of the timeless
Kings and legends never die
We just transition and live forever

"THE LEGACY OF A POET"

The world is finally paying attention
To what a king like me is cooking in the kitchen
My whole vibe is different
Guaranteed to make a difference
Ooooo I'm about to kill' em
My mouth is the pistol
And my tongue is the trigger
Crowning men as kings no longer nigga
Nigga, nigga lets eliminate that term out your temple
When I speak through the bass I make the world tremble
Touching souls like hymnals
Surrounded around clashing cymbals
My reign will always be remembered
My rule will never be hindered
My legacy is to be continued
Given God all the gratitude
That is how I pay tribute
He turned my gray skies into clear and beautiful blues
He gave me a unique rhythm so I can blessed the world with these
poetic tunes
I had to create a space because no one would make room
I came in real smooth
I moved real cool
My style
Issa whole vibe
I can never be denied
Where there's smoke theirs fire
All my enemies they run and hide
The world has been awakened by a king from the west side

I have the keys of wisdom and knowledge
No lullabies
When I die
Its see you later, no goodbyes
Kings and legends never die
We just multiply
And crossover to the other side

"WELCOME TO BIRMINGHAM"

Welcome to Birmingham
The Magic City
A place of history
Division and unity
Love and envy
Friends and enemies
A place of silent villages and unsolved mysteries
The home of Bam, Major, Jurnee and Cupcake McKinney
Welcome to Birmingham
The Magic City
The place of single mothers with at least two children
Where there's a lack of men in the village
Desperately in need of accountability
Welcome to Birmingham
The Magic City
Where on the outer skirts lives white privilege and white
supremacy
Where you must not exceed the speed limit
When you leave outside the inner cities limits
Welcome to Birmingham
The Magic City
Where progress lies at the hands of the people
Welcome to Birmingham
The Magic City
Where churches are on every corner and some gain millions
And are silent on putting an end to racism
Welcome to Birmingham
The Magic City
The place of many creatives, leaders and imperfect people

Welcome to Birmingham
The Magic City
Where between the suburbs and the hood
There is a lot of good and there is a lot of evil
Welcome to Birmingham
The Magic City
Where in times of testing and trials we know how to come
together
And there is a will to want to do better
Welcome to Birmingham
The Magic City
Where lately there has been a slight applying of pressure
A slight break in to the movie and music industries
A cutting out of the middle man
Ownership of masters and royalties from streams
Success lies at the hands of the people; that's independent
Welcome to Birmingham
The Magic City
Where there has been, so many losses
That our only option now is to win
Its not about how you began, its about how you end
Welcome to Birmingham
Where the truth of the Magic lies within

"I AM BIRMINGHAM"

I am Birmingham
The rising voice of the people
A place of struggle
A place of hustle
A place of murders
A place of high hurdles
A place where its hard to trust men
Where friends turn to foes
And foes turn to friends
We all are dying to win
We all are crabs fighting to escape from a bucket
Trying to keep hold of our souls
And not become a puppet
Gun shots ring out in the night
And crowds stand around to see what the ruckus is about
A mother cries out loud
Leaning over her child
Whose journey ended at 18 miles
With no protest or pump fists standing black and proud
This life is a marathon
You can run it or slow down and walk it out
But whatever you do don't remain on the couch
The journey has already been mapped out
And don't jump of the porch too fast
Because that's how many young niggas end up breathing their last
Too many bright futures have become past
This life that we live, is but a grain of sand slipping
away through an hourglass
Your soul or fame?

Is the price really worth having the bag?

"I AM B' HAM"

I am B' Ham
Alabama is the trending topic
The voices of good trouble
Diamonds beneath the rubble
We are no stranger to struggle
We are B' Ham
The mega city for locals blowing up
The kings and queens of the south
We show out when we show up
It's time to put homicides
Being number 5 in crime
And living gangstafied
Behind us
And gentrify
The minds of the marginalized
Unifying against those who attempt to neutralize and ostracize
The systematically victimized
The foolish things of the world
Putting to shame the wise things
That claim to be woke with closed eyes
Now listen as I talk my talk
With an open mind
Being young, gifted and black has always been
And will be throughout the ages of time
There's no end to our melanated skin that we live in on a day to
day basis
That's being judge by unjust laws and court cases
They got us all messed up
Inequalities

police brutality
and the mass incarceration of black males in a jail cell
We are living in a world of hell
I'm trying to redirect you to Heavens stairwell
Give you freedom with a double dose of truth everybody is afraid
to tell
From the roots deeply rooted in me
And hopefully
You want depart from it
Being poor you have a state of realness
Being rich will lift you from humility
My hope is that you don't drift to far from it

"DID YOU KNOW"

Did you know
That in 87 Mary would birth a king
Born to show the people the way in a time that their asking
What's Going on?
Crying Lord Mercy, Mercy me in the storm
Things ain't what they use be
Picket signs and police brutality
All the young brothers are dying in our communities
Where is the elderly man's legacy
The cry of a young man's heart is will someone please father me
It takes a village to raise a child, but the state of the village bothers
me
This is the heart of my artistry
What has happened to the unity in our communities
We all used to be like family
Now it seems like all we know is struggle and tragedy
No snitch policies got us walking on casually
From slaves ships, to cotton fields, to the trap house, to the
penitentiary
These chains we were born in, but far from what we was born to
be
We were destined to be kings and queens
Ruling every land with dominion and authority
Every man controls his own destiny
Its up to you to get up, get out and make it happen
With no complaining
Maintaining a consistent hustle
Being persistent in the struggle
Persevering through the tuggle

Squashing beefs and holding no grudges
Loving all men because its only God that can judge you and me
Love is the only remedy that will set humanity free
And break these chains off of our mentality
Bridging the gap between warring families
My words are vital to our communities
To elevate us higher than where we are
Our rightful place is through the galaxies way beyond the stars
Far away from planet Earth
Where time clocks don't exist
And everything is timeless..
Hits..

"CHILDHOODS ARE CLASSIC"

This is a classic throwback
When I was 33 years younger
And humble
I'm still humble
Quiet with a silent rumble
I got a story to tell
Real life no fairy tales
About a young king
From Avenue Lee in West End
87 my legacy began
It all started with Mary and Edward Glenn
My sis and years later Mo Mo moved in
The vital parts of my up bringing
Was my family
And most importantly
How my parents rooted God in me
Every Sunday we got up early heading to T.O.P
Where Pastor Raines preached
I remember those Sundays when we use to fellowship and eat
We had a feast
I remember hallelujah nights and youth shut ins
I can never forget back then
As a child we were innocent children
I love reminiscing on way back when
When I was a child in West End
I remember neighborhood friends
When Lil Mike taught me to ride a bike
When me, Eric and Nuke use to hoop
When I went to Price and then Arrington Middle School

When my bro Ced use to cut up and act a fool
He was cool
I can't believe hes gone
He was 30 years too young
My heart goes out to Derrick, Trina and Von
To Your wife, daughter and sons
Always keep God first and pray on
It's so many others to speak on
My list is way too long
To write in this poem
Its crazy how fast life goes on
Yesterday we was young
Today were tryna hold our own
Mama always told me
There will be days like this
Don't rush your days
Cause years later
You will get caught in the bliss
Wishing you could relive
Those childhood days
Those days that made us legendary..
That's indeed a precious gift
Always apart of you and me..
To be forever cherished..
In our memory..

"BACK TO THE FUTURE"

Sometimes I wish
I could time travel and trip
Relive this bliss and reminisce
When I was a kid
On Avenue Lee
In West End
The life of me
The upbringings of a king
The makings of history
It was..
My mom and dad
My sister, Mo-Mo and me
We never had it all
But we had many things
Good food on the table
Mo-Mo cooking neck bones and collard greens
Meals that you put your foot in
With chocolate or lemon supreme birthday cakes
She had recipes and prayers to shape kings and queens
Southern roots in Vernon and Suligent
No chef can touch the cooking
Of Mo-Mo, Cousin Pearline, Aunt Dorothy and Aunt Tea
The soul of the family
We need back our traditions
Because the future of our children
Depends on it
Get money
Buy the land
So they can own it

Its nothing like the love you feel in the country
In Mississippi, Vernon, Fayette and Suligent
We can turn open fields into something
Gain millions
Make investments
Take back ours from those rich white southerners
Bring to the country Wakanda, Africa
Its easier said than done
We gotta make them understand that Mo-Mo and Paw-Paws
hands mattered
And still matters
To this day..

"DEAR MAMA"

They say to give roses to those you love while there still living
Well..
This is my rose to the one that's the reason for my existence
Whose prayers are behind every breath that I'm breathing
For all my stubborn ways please forgive me
I thank you for your love and your wisdom
Even though you think that I'm never listening
If I ruled the world I would give you half a billion
Pay all your bills and give you a new kidney
I want you with me for an eternity
Watch me get marry and lead a family
Blessed is your name and great will be your legacy
If there was no you in this world that would be vanity
You are a gift to all humanity
You did all you could for your family
With the little that you were given
But you still kept a hot meal in the kitchen
It's your love and wisdom
That flows through every word that I have written
Engulfed into my very heart beat
When the streets feel me
They feel you to because I carry you inside of me
You are victory
In a world of impossibilities
You raised a black man that's free with no felonies
That's something to be proud about
Your seed will be forever deeply rooted in me
Passed down to my future child
Your faith is a blueprint for me to stand strong in every trial

Because of you I could never throw in the towel
The race is not to the swift, nor the battle to the strong, but to you
continue to run your marathon
No matter how many miles
No matter how weary and tired
Knowing at the end you will forever shine
Leaving everything that tried to hold you down..
Far behind..

"JUST BEING ME"

I'm just being me
My soul underneath my own skin
That makes me independent and free
Just be you, while I be me
We don't need anymore clones in society
Or the music industry
There's too many look a likes
Sound a likes
In the 90s everybody wanted to be like Mike
To do the right thing
Is to do your own thing
Think different
Speak different
Live different
Look different
Pave your own lane
Ride your own wave
Let the world see you
Uniquely crafted from Gods likeness
You are not meant for everyone's liking
Children of God don't need squads, cliques and many side kicks
Greatness isn't always the first round draft pick
The wealthiest are not always those that appear rich
You must be proud of what God handmade you to be
Healthy
Whole
Free
You're truly blessed
If you have breath

And a warm home to lay your body to rest
Be happy and thankful
Even if you have less
Until more is acquired

"LEGENDARY"

Legendary
Is what I was born to be
To awaken souls with my artistry
Is a vital part of my destiny
The ability
To paint vivid pictures
Was inherited
Pass down from my mother
To my sister and me
I am poetry
Stanzas and mantras flowing through my veins
Words that reflect the times
From Birmingham and beyond
Let the music play
Dance to the rhythm of the tribal drums
Our words unlocked the door to our freedom
Young, gifted, black and strong
We are the next generation of John Lewis and Nina Simone
We bare a new song
Our legacy will forever live on
America is the place we belong
The land our great grandfathers tilled on
The New Jerusalem is our ancestral home
We are God manifested in human form
The royal and the righteous ones
The home of Yahshua the Son
Our soul has been burdened from deep wounds and battle scars
Hated in a nation filled with deep roots of racism
Because we are melanated

Hated by people that claim to serve the God that created the
melanated
When they to were created by the same God that created the
melanated
That's what makes us all related
We are one humans race
A virally infected population
That's in need of saving

"THE BALLAD OF A POET"

Being a poet means something
I was born to keep souls jumping
While the bass thumping
Alabama the world bumping
The dawn of a new Space Age
Among Star ships and Rockets
Trying not to loose these last two dollars in my pockets
The life of an artist
On the road to stardom
Music is therapy
A rapid release from postpartum
Into the realm of the unforgotten
Time is platinum
And is eternity is gold
Only feed the mind
What touches the soul
We are God in the flesh
And our lives are the Gospel for a world ghetto
No hype men, No yes men
The greatest of all men
Are those that roll solo
And live mellow
Only arrogant men stumble
Be proud, black, powerful and humble
Though life is a concrete jungle
Among the lions, the wolves and the piranhas
And a few snakes in the grass
Let your words echo the world like a gun blast
Be yourself, without a mask

Forever you will last
Beyond the sand in your hourglass
Eternity is longer than what an hour last
You are the future even when you're past
A lighthouse blazing for many paths
In a world engulfed with darkness
A treacherous journey to embark on
But you must carry on
There will be trials along the way
But after every dark night
After every gray sky
There will be brighter days
Surrounded by clear and beautiful blues
The awakening of the soul
You are the greatest story ever told
You must show them who you truly are
A born legend and a star

"KING TALK PT. 1"

I spit pure dope
I'm about ten kilos
Take a hit line for line
Stimulate your mind
Let's go where it ain't no time
Just the stars and forever
Our reign is forever
We don't never die
We just transition
Into another realm of existence
I can double up and make a million
But it want go with me
That's to leave
For my seeds living
I am the blueprint
A footprint in the sand
A rendition to "grandmas hands"
We don't dance no more
All we do is this
Get up, get out and drop hits
Hold on to your soul
Cause contracts only make "Massa" rich
They write a check then control you like Willie Lynch
Give you a ghost writer
You only get more if your skin lighter
And when you finally break away
You turn freedom fighter
With little time left
Go get yo classics off the shelf

Perfect your flow
Protect your soul
And own masters
Be greater than King
Be greater than Nip
Be even greater than Tip
Be even more legend than Gladys Knight and the Pips
Always pulling deep from your soul
Give and give some more
Live and live some more
Before its your time to go
You only get one life, one soul
You must make every punch count
Theirs no time to lounge around
A marathon is ten toes on the ground

"KING TALK PT. 2"

Born in 87
With the sound of Heaven
Mama carried a legend
Every drop is pure evidence
To sleep on me
Is the world's biggest regret
The underrated
And the underestimated
Are viewed as the biggest threat
I come from
The West side of the slums
Where if you impose the threat of success
Inner hate will have you killed
Its really real
In the field
It's a struggle to survive
And a fight to live
If you have no peace
You will have no sleep
If you have no love
Theirs no chances of forgiveness
Without love there is no reach for the masses of people
You have been given
The ability to be informative
Changing the narratives
Demolishing all ignorance
Making an absolute difference
Remain consistent
Remain persistent

Be resistant
Stand firm against society's interference
Be the voice for the prison systems
Be freedom for those suffering from mental illness
Stand with resilience
Always be different
Don't follow crowds
Lead the crowds
Hold your head up
And walk proud
Never throw in the towel
There are many souls that are depending on your every mile
So run wise
But never stop running
Victory only comes to those that keep running
Discovery only comes to those that are consistently seen
We are the solution to the worlds issues
As the marathon continues

"THE BLACK LOVE STORY"

Black woman you are beautiful
Light skinned or dark complexion
I love the shade of your melanin
The way your skin reflects from the sun rays
It's an honor to call you forever my lady
Through sexual healings we drive each other crazy
My one and only lady
You're one of the greatest gifts God gave me
I love the way you walk up to me
And how you wear your crown proudly
You're a legend
You're a classic
If black was a drug I would be an attic
Your high is everlasting
You and I are royalty
It's an honor to be called your majesty
Great is our legacy
Our seed will outnumber the stars in the sky and the sand on the
sea shore
What you need I'll give you more and more
You are my Cherie Amour
I am king to the core
A knight in shining armor
With a double edged sword
Always ready for war
Theirs no need to fear
Just blow the trumpet
Just sound the alarm
And I will be there

No matter how far
You are
And forever you will be
My shining star
All praises to Yah
Our Creator
The Great and Mighty God
Through His Power I'll grant you every wish that you wish upon
the stars
We can even traveled the universe, rename all the planets and the
stars
Defy all of gravity laws
Our reign will be remembered forever by those near and far

"THIS TYPE LOVE (MORE THAN A FEELING)"

I'm searching for love
One out of a billion women
In synced with one anothers energy
My one and only lady
Impressed with my word play
Snapping her fingers
Telling her friends
He drives me crazy
I love his style
And Hes a whole vibe
This type love
Is more than a feeling
More than sexual healings
We vibe well
This type love will make you climax just to listen
As we put aside differences
As we trade words of wisdom
Washing feet is a way to keep a flame kindled
Quality time
A woman's gotta have it
Something real
A genuine feel
A little tenderness
Every man needs an everlasting friend
From now into his golden years
This is a mans world
But it would be nothing without a woman or a girl

Worth more than fine diamonds and Pearl's
Give her the world
Let your presence give her chills and make her toes curl
Make her feel that she is the greatest being to ever walk the Earth
Lighten the load of the curse
Be the peace she needs
From bearing your seed
Through child birth
Make her feel her value
And understand her worth
Shes valued
Shes queen
And shes worth the wait

"LIGHTHOUSE"

The south got something to say
We all have our individual stories to tell
We must be consistent
Stand persistent
Until the world begins to listen
Write down your vision
Never abort mission
Breath is evidence of a life that's purpose driven
In the words of John Jr.
Let's light it up for the city one time
Let's shine real bright til they recognize our existence
Waking the world up from the deepest coma
Alabama it's about time y'all start spitting
Poets it's about time y'all start really speaking
A voiceless people are looking for a beacon
Incarcerated minds are daydreaming of what freedom looks like
Let's take a moment of silence
Hear there souls cry
A voiceless people are looking for a leader
One single person that will make a difference
The artist pays the price
So that you want have to pay
Just remain calm and listen to there wisdom
Everyday life contains lessons
Its vital that we start learning
The knowledge that we gain will enhance our journey
The legends of old are our motivation to keep running
The marathon continues throughout the generations to come
Our legacy is our baton

Our Melanin is magic
With a glow that shines bright as the Sun

"NO MORE COMFORT ZONES"

Respect to Tennessee
Respect to California
Respect to Louisiana
Respect to Atlanta
But its time for Alabama
The heartbeat of the south
The home of Eddie Kendricks and the Dirty Boys
Birmingham J and Rich Boy
Chika and Translee
Bam Bam and Northside Weezy
Let history Remember Doe B
John Jr. And Rocki
Our life is our artistry
No eye has seen
And no ear has heard
True creativity
Until you've heard Devonta Ravizee
And the song of Ashley Sankey
Kallie Skys and Harmonee
Legends that could never be bought

With no amount of Money
Music for the soul
To get you through when you have nothing
Expecting for something
We are all poets
Searching for rhyme schemes
To silence the pistol play

So the world may hear what the south has to say
Let the music play on
From dusk to dawn
Our voices are our freedom song
Freedom from mental illness
Freedom for the boy that's calls the trap his home
Freedom for a single mothers home
We control the tone
Together we are one song
We bring the world a different sound
Our masters we own
Catalogs of new songs
Books with new poems
Therapy through the storms
Blow the trumpet
Dance to the rhythm of the tribal drums
Today is the day that Alabama is finally on..
Forever..
No more Comfort Zones..

"TIRED"

Have you every been so tired?
Tired of hearing the same things over again
America has no valid excuse over what happens daily
How much they value our organs
How the world turns there back on trafficking humans
Brothas and sistas killing each other in close proximity in our
community
Another unarmed black civilian becomes a victim of police
brutality
Young white Americans turns vigilante
Walks pass the police casually
Then gets apprehended peacefully
How can you confuse murder with patriotism
Ignore blatant racism
Surrounded by silent preachers and Christians
Prefer private reconciliation meetings
Over publicly renouncing hatred and racism
If the power is in the people why must we put faith in politicians
To rid us of all the evil isms
Seems like no matter who occupies the building
We are still living in the same conditions
Can we all agree that the only solution is a change of heart within
an individual
America has never been indivisible; given justice to all
That statement is so hypocritical
On a stolen land that was "supposedly" founded on biblical
principles
Systematically oppressing and brutally apprehending Yahushas
holy temple

I know that just went over your temple
They been ostracizing, neutralizing and trying to eliminate us
from human existence
We shouldn't have to explain our human experience over and
over again
The blue remains free due to a goofy claim of insufficient
evidence
But we get 20 years for inhaling herbal medication and exhaling
the stress
Or locked away for popping a government seal and failing a
breathe test
Please Mr. Officer I'm already handcuffed so why is your knee still
on my neck
As I can't breathe, as 9 minutes turns into seconds
Again I say, "can we all agree that the only solution is a change of
heart within an individual"
The only progress is self progress
To become better human beings
So that we may digress
And live peacefully again

"AMERICAN HYPOCRISY"

Its a shame
The world still needs to be educated
About the history of the melanated
It started with over 400 years of slavery
And then, over 50 years of being segregated
The year is 2021 and the bloodline of our ancestors still haven't
received respiration's
America was built by black hands,
And police brutality
And systemic racism is how they reciprocate
Always, Ostracized and neutralized when we congregate
I can't breathe, I think I'm about to suffocate
How can we get a slice of this American Pie, when many of us
can't even have a dinner plate
We've tried to survive off of 7.25 for far too long
Breaking our backbones
Its about time we gain and see change as creation groans from
these hunger pains
Were gaining momentum
But were slowed down by political agendas
I see the contracts, but what are the terms and conditions
Within the right and the left there are common enemies
I'm looking to the Heavens above asking God for love and energy
So I can spread the vibe throughout our communities
Expressing the importance of nonprofits and black owned
businesses
Its much deeper than voting and changing policies
And how they police society
You can give rights, change laws and implement new policies

But it want effect humanities individuality
The root cause of American hypocrisy
Only the reunification of God with humanity, is the
meaning of standing on the correct side of history

"JEALOUSY + ENVY"

Its all love and trust when you're in the same position
When you haven't yet acquired the fame and the riches
The fame and the riches of the world
Will turn friends into one another's opposition
The transition into a cold hearted individual
Jealousy + Envy = lack of men in the village
Dead or living out a prison sentence
And it happens to women too
Jealousy + Envy doesn't discriminate against who it gets into
Just be sure it doesn't get into you
It appears when you side eye or turn your nose up into a frown
Followed by a selfish grin that can lead you to putting a friend into
the ground
All because one decided to lift his boots off the ground
Getting his back from against the wall And you're afraid that
you're about to be left behind
Love doesn't live when you're on the grind
Jealousy + Envy begins in the mind
Then it taints the soul
Jealousy + Envy doesn't easily let go, when you're under its grip
It usually leads you to a self-destructive end
A loss of family and friends

"UNIVERSAL LOVE"

Love makes the world go round
Love is a universal sound
Love is a language from above
Love was sent with love
All of humanity was made in love
So all humanity must return the love
There is no face or race with love
Our seeds we must grow up in love
That's how we destroy hate with love
We must spread knowledge when we come up
That's how we spread the love
Love is how many will follow us
Love transforms I, into we and then into us
When we unite in love
Its impossible for the world to stop us
Love is a powerful force in us
We are much stronger when is us
The System vs. Us
If Gods love is in us
Who can stand up against us
Without Gods love we are defenseless
Where there is no love there can be no trust
And where there is no love there can be know exchange of
wisdom
Without love theirs less victors and more victims
That's why theirs so many prison systems
Because the enemy knows in freedom There is a whole lot of love
to be given
Lack of love is why the judge will hold a grudge and give you a life

sentence
Lack of love will transform a king, to a nigga to a straight up
menace
If you wanna change all things in the world
Reach up to the Heavens above
And grab a hold of love
And you will become different
Making an absolute difference

"FREE WRITE SESSION 1"

My deepest desire is to inspire
Speak the truth real, full of zeal and passion..
Make the people feel my words
Realize my worth
Before I'm buried underneath the dirt
Working overtime to change the narratives
You can't tell everybody your vision and dreams because they will
try and assassinate your character
You gotta believe in yourself and keep God first, that is the
common factors
You gotta be true to yourself and never become an actor
You gotta educate yourself to break away from the chains that
hold you bound to a master
You gotta face your problems because that's a giant of a disaster
that's waiting to happen
You gotta hide yourself away with God to drown out the paparazzi
and the laughter
I wanted the world to hear the value in my words so I chose to
speak over rapping
Getting you lost in the deepest melodies
It is our voices that shakes the highest heaven-lies
Pulling lost souls out of the darkest pits and the deepest valleys
We matter and we possess value
We must not thrive off of accolades and flattery
That's isn't needed if you believe that you are a powerful force to
be reckoned with
No one can thwart your power or ability..
To be great..
To be kinged..

To be queened..
To be legend..
To be classic..
To have a name that will last forever..
Our rule..
Our reign..
Will last forever..
No human can stand against.. because there is a God that resides
within..
He's been there since the ages first began and He will always be to
the ends of the eARTh
We were place here to lift up every curse..
Off of those who are weak..
And to cause every proud man to become humbled and meek
We've been oppressed and marginalized, but not defeated..
We now have hope, that we can now breathe again
I hope that my every word will be a planted seed into the hearts of
men
To restore love again
Transforming enemies to friends
Fulfilling a demanding cry for unity
Within our communities
This I speak into existence
On behalf of our young seeds
Every word that I speak, I will speak as if though it will be the last
words you will ever hear from a king
The world will know of my existence and my reign as supreme

"FREE WRITE SESSION 2"

I close my eyes
Searching the deep inner depths of my soul for the perfect rhyme
The greatest words that hold no frame of time
Words that will stick to the human mind
Pushing the human race ahead of time
We've been promised 70 years, that's 613,000 hours of time
24 hours in one day to achieve a successful grind
All we have is time
And its slips away fast
No one can flip there own hourglass
We must work consistently, diligently and urgently on our daily
task
Preparing a legacy that will last forever
Forever is truly a mighty long time
It takes time to shine
It takes time to manifest your glow
In a world that's dark and cold
In a society that wants control over your soul
Mind, will and emotions
Your peace you must keep a tight grip on
Never letting go
Beware of who you stroll with
Never being afraid to take the lonely road
Build your own Avenue
Stack up your revenue
Understand that you are valuable
You are powerful
Immeasurable
Your greatness and your ability goes far beyond what the eye can

see
Theirs no limits or statutes on what you could be
You can be anything that your heart desires to be
All you gotta do is believe
And jump no matter how high
And dive in no matter how deep
Knowing that every good thing comes from those that believe
You are a light for all to see
Someone needs your energy
Your vibe and positivity
In every community
And in our society
You were made to spread love and inner peace
Creating spaces of forgiveness among enemies

"LEGENDS"

We must pay homage
To those that came before us
Those who laid out blueprints
Who left footprints in the sand
Those who showed us the power of wealth and bands
Those who gave us the keys to fame
Left us life lessons to keep us sane
Through the struggles, the rain and the pain
Until we reach our promised land
We as a people will get to the promised land
With a dance like Micheal Jackson
With a groove like James Brown
Our voices are renditions of that classic Motown sound
With a ray of sunshine
On a cloudy day
When it's cold outside
I've got the month of May
I guess you can say
What can make me feel this way
I can hear the sounds of Martha and the Vandellas
Diana Ross and the Supremes
Smokie had the Tempts sounding like some true kings
Jr Walker, Ron Isley and the Isley Brothers
Possessed voices like no other
Marvin Gaye spoke into the souls of those in the Inner City with
blues
In a time when Malcolm X said that your mind is the tool
By any means necessary this world we will rule
With a Awnaw hell nawl like Nappy Roots

The blacker the berry the sweeter the juice
The darker the flesh the deeper the roots
To our roots we must remain true
Knocking down the trees that bares strange fruit
Those trees that Nina Simone sung about with blood on the leaves
From her planted seeds grew a Baby Rose from the cracks of the
concrete
It was those that marched with sores on their feet
To open up doors for Ball and G
Bun and Pimp
Cole and Krit
Long before you and I ever came to exist
The first black panther rose up with one pumped fist
With free healthcare and bags of groceries
A black wall street type of society
The grass roots of Kobe Bryant's Mamba Mentality
Out of the heart the mouth speaks the power of wealth and
knowledge to collect bands
A sudden freedom from a long time struggle
Love and Peace to the Late Great Nipsey Hussle
We are all on a Marathon run..
We must continue to run on..
As life goes on..

"SEASONS"

Our Father
who art in heaven
hallowed be thy name
Thy kingdom come
Thy will be done
on earth
as it is in heaven
Let all men bow and give reverence
Let us pray more than ask questions
Let us learn from past lessons
Teaching our seeds to value legacy
To live life unforgettable
Every moment is treasure-able
Time is platinum
And eternity is gold
How you live your life
Effects your soul
What does it profit a man
To gain this world
And loose his soul
Hold on to your soul
Never selling your soul
Never be afraid to tell a man no
Stand firm
Always Listen and discern
If your dreams are slow motion
Just be patient
And wait your turn
Slow seasons

Happen for a reason
But you must keep going
You must keep believing
Many souls need you
Many are depending on you
To make it out your seasons
Your destiny
Just might be and open door to someones freedom
Humanity is dependant on you and me
We are a visual of the God they need to see
Because He lives through you and me
Yahshua..
Jesus..
He is..
Love..
Peace..
And Freedom..

THANK YOU

I would like to first thank God the Father of Yahshua my health, my strength, my source and for my abilty to write. I will like to thank my mother and my father for all the love and wisdom they have poured into me throughout my 33 years of living. I will like to send out a special thank you to the city that bred me, Birmingham, Alabama and all that will purchase this book. I hope that my words will find a special place in your hearts.

ABOUT THE AUTHOR

About The Author

Jamil, also known as, "B' Ham's Poet", or "The Peoples Poet", is an American poet. His desire is to be not just a poet, but a catalyst for change and a beacon of hope for many. Jamil's literary work is noted for addressing contemporary social issues and inequalities that plague inner cities.

Made in the USA
Columbia, SC
05 October 2022

68689934R00035